MW01595339

# 33 Life Lessons

*Life Experiences
that Have Enabled My Growth*

# Quortni Fambro

This book is dedicated to you.
You matter and so do your ambitions!

# CONTENTS

# PREFACE

Turning 33 has inspired me and provided clarity in many ways. As I looked further into the meaning of the number 33, the life shift I felt made sense. According to some research, here are a few random facts I found about the meaning of the number 33:

- In numerology, **33** is considered a "master number." It radiates harmonious and caring energy, emphasizing the importance of helping others and fostering unity.
- The number **33** promotes creativity and expression, encouraging you to let your artistic side shine (the inspiration I felt to write this book)!
- This period in life can be profoundly impactful, much like it was for historical and spiritual figures such as Jesus Christ. For many, 33 represents a blend of self-awareness, career maturity, and deeper relationships, making it a unique and meaningful time.
- In the Bible, the number 33 is associated with **divine favor, blessings, and the Holy Trinity**. It's also linked to God keeping his promises.

- Some say it is because Jesus died at 33, while others say it's because 33 is when we reach our physical and intellectual peaks. Research has found that age 33 is apparently also when we are happiest. Naturally, I felt a weight of expectation as this pivotal birthday arrived.
- 33 is pretty unique. Number 33 is a Master Number (Master Teacher) and resonates with the energies of compassion, blessings, inspiration, honesty, discipline, bravery and courage. Number 33 tells us that 'all things are possible'. 33 is also the number that symbolizes 'guidance'.
- The 33 angel number means anything is possible.

# No Other Person Will Prioritize You More than Yourself

I have grown to learn that prioritizing myself is of the utmost importance in most aspects of my life. I am a very ambitious person, and I am the only one who can see my vision in the way it is meant to be seen. When you are in the process of working towards a goal, you may not have time to give excessive energy to others, because focus requires direction and a high level of attention to detail that can only be derived from a tad bit of selfishness. I am a single woman, with no spouse, and no children, which makes it easier to accomplish certain goals. Ambition is a great characteristic to have but understand that it also has an effect on other areas of life.

As I stated, I am not married and I do not have a family, partially because I have prioritized myself and the things I aspire to accomplish, which takes time away from focusing on the thought of settling into life's formalities. For example, my professional endeavors have taken me to positions in law enforcement, the armed forces, and frequent relocations. With that comes a level of instability that has taken a toll on my options in men. I find it is difficult to find a man who is willing to follow and support a woman's career, compared to a man finding a woman who will follow him through his life's journey. I understand that there are certain traditions that may never be broken, but this can be a side effect of self-prioritization. Your personal life may take longer to be established; however, all things happen in the time they are preordained.

Understand that all good things are not always fun. Growth is knowing when to go against the current of life, and when to let life flow in its own direction to deliver you to your intended destination. When you prioritize what's best for you and not what you want, you'll be more understanding of why you took certain losses, and why the thing you most wanted to avoid turned out to be the best option for you and your life. Be patient. Be decisive. Prioritize based on logic, not emotion.

# LESSON 2

# APOLOGIZE, BUT DON'T COMPROMISE

Sometimes life brings about frustrations and we don't handle things in the best way. Emotions are a part of us, as we are social beings constantly going through the ebbs and flows of life. Romantic relationships, familial relationships, and friendships all have the ability to bring things out of us that we wouldn't normally feel. When these instances occur, it is okay to be remorseful about your actions if you overreacted and behaved in an uncharacteristic way, and sometimes a sincere apology can invoke healing for the other party. However, even if you apologize, have the integrity to maintain the passion you had for your initial feelings. My mother told me early on in life that the first reaction is typically the right one. What that means is, we all have intuition that guides us to feel the way we do about certain situations, or people, or even about the things that have not happened yet. Although you may be sincerely apologetic about your actions, it is okay to not compromise the way you think or feel.

This is a lesson I feel is very important, because as a caring and compassionate individual, I have been faced with instances where I thought it would be better to put the feelings of someone else above what I was feeling to keep the peace, but I realize that this action is often one that builds against you as you go along. This means that people will sometimes remember certain instances and attempt to replicate their dominance over your stance. They may bring up a time when you "changed your mind" because they assumed you felt you were wrong, but in reality, it was a simple gesture of kindness. In my opinion it is okay to have a disagreement, but I don't agree that you should allow people to discredit you based on an apology.

## LESSON 3

# NEVER BE ENAMORED OF COMPANIONSHIP, INSTEAD BE FOCUSED ON LOGIC

As we get older, we fall in love with the idea of love. There are so many pressures and societal conditions we get caught up in as we age, especially women. We feel as though we are supposed to have it all figured out by a certain age, and many people even feel like failures if they are not married with a family once they reach their 30's. However, I've learned that life always happens as it should. Everything that is meant for us will happen in the proper time. Although I know better, I often romanticize the idea of men once we start dating, mentally planning things out, expecting everything to fall into the place I have set for it in my mind. Now that I've grown in age and as a person, I now have the logic to slow my passion in order to remain in logic. Companionship is important to us as humans, more than some people like to admit. But, in the process of finding your person, I encourage you to remain in a calm mindset free of sensual haze, the thought of potential love, and instead look at the person you are pursuing from a commonsensical standpoint. Analyze their behavior, look intently at your ability to tolerate the things about them you may not like, dissect their abilities to keep their word and follow through, pay attention to how they treat you when they're upset, and give yourself time to provide an overall break down of what you genuinely believe a future looks like for the two of you if you decide to commit.

One question I heard someone say to ask oneself when deciding on a love interest is; if this person never changes, would I be happy with my decision? I think that question is impactful because it encompasses the ability to question a reality that is not always considered when we are in a love trance. Life seems to be the most unexpected in matters of the heart. Remember, be enamored of the realism, think through your feelings before you commit to anything.

# Expect the Unexpected from People, Places, and Things

Have you ever been so sure about something that you were fully committed to it, went above and beyond to ensure that it happened, only to find that it was in fact not the right path for you? Whether it was because you failed at it, or simply because fate decided that you were not eligible. Either way, I have experienced both, and I now have gotten comfortable with the idea of expecting the unexpected. Rolling with the punches of life is a healthy skill to maintain because I think it keeps you aware of all possibilities. I think disappoint can be a great tool towards success, if properly managed and cultivated into the hard work and dedication necessary to later overcome the past failures. Feelings of excitement, anger, happiness, and even anxiousness are all fleeting. Which means we cannot live our lives based on how we feel in the moment. Life takes us through so many changes; becoming spouses or parents, losing loved ones, getting laid off, moving to new places, taking on more responsibility at work, growing out of friendships, breakups, experiencing unexpected traumas, etc. Life is so unpredictable that it is only right to think about the things we don't want to consider and be prepared for the possible outcomes. One thing that has taken me the most time to adjust to in my life, is the fact that people are allowed to change their minds about things that involve you. Understand that people are all different and we don't always handle things similarly. Time is the most valuable thing we have; it allows for healing, growth, separation, and enjoyment. I think it is worth it to put your faith in time as it is the only thing that is undetermined yet passes by you daily. The unexpected things in life challenge our growth as individuals and can allow us to become better once we understand that we cannot avoid them.

# Be Excited About All of Your Accomplishments, Even the Small Ones

I think people are excited about the things they accomplish, only if they feel as though it is being recognized by others. People have anticipations of how many people will acknowledge them, what they will gain because of their success, and maybe even how they will grow in status. I rarely see people be proud of what they've achieved for the sake of being fulfilled, but I have made it my duty to practice being genuinely satisfied with the accomplishing my goals. In my personal life, I have decided to take time to set goals annually and feel the gratitude associated with reaching them. As a single individual, I am my biggest fan! I realize as you get older, achievements are mostly shared with the person you are in a relationship with, or your immediate family. As you age, people aren't really concerned about what you're doing in life, unless it's something negative they can talk about. People seem to enjoy controversy. In order to avoid getting involved in other people's misery, stay focused on the course to your success. Any forward step in life is major no matter how big or small the impact is. Be proud of your talents, there are people who will never accomplish the things you have already finished succeeding at.

# MAINTAIN A SENSE OF WONDER

Children are so full of intrigue and curiosity because they are constantly trying to learn the world around them. They often continue to do things out of ignorance, even when they are told not to, or experience pain. I am not suggesting that you behave irrationally and do things that get you hurt, but I am saying maintaining an optimistic childlike wonder can be healthy. Take the time to explore new things and places, be open to unlearning old habits, or learn new skills. Sometimes as we age, we get comfortable and complacent with our personal norms. Having a routine is nice, but sometimes taking healthy risks opens the doors for new opportunities. A sense of wonder brings newness and excitement to life that can only be realized when you try new things. Being open is one of the healthiest experiences in life, in my opinion. Sometimes the idea of what we want is closer than we think if we just get started. From my experience, I can pinpoint the moment I became a bit overly cautious, and I would say that was at the age of 28. Prior to then, I was so ready to go skydiving as an activity for my birthday, I wanted to travel abroad solo, and I was aware of possible dangers, but I was fearless. Now, I am still fearless. But, everything I do is with reason and I weigh the pros and cons of my actions; even in leisure. I believe as we grow older we should be more aware of potential dangers, but that doesn't mean to eliminate the action of taking risks; your risk taking just needs to be reframed. Even people with children who want to still live an exciting life, I think it is possible to manage both your "personal" life and being a parent. I encourage you all to never lose your sense of wonder, it is what makes us all unique.

# AGE DOES NOT DETERMINE HOW SUCCESSFUL YOU ARE OR WHERE YOU SHOULD BE IN LIFE

Age seems to be a factor we stress about both individually and in society. As we age, it seems we tend to feel rushed to accomplish all we want before we get "old". The thing is, death has no age, and it is something unexpected most of the time. Stressing about what you have not done in relation to your age is an unhealthy outlook on life, and it only feeds into a negative outlook on life. As a woman, I have had moments where I have felt maternal, and felt I was prepared to be married and have a child. Although these are valid thoughts and feelings, my timing is not in my control. What I mean by this is, things always happen as they should, and as someone who believes in Christianity, I know that everything happens on God's timing. I have never felt like a failure as it relates to my personal life, but I have felt as though I should have had these things established at my age. After about three years of feeling I was on a time crunch, I have made a conscious effort to focus on living life responsibly and productively and accomplishing things professionally until it is my opportunity to be a wife and mother. I am proud of the things I have accomplished in my life, and I believe it is important to never diminish anything; what you consider to be a small feat, others are hoping to one day achieve! With age should come some wisdom and discernment. Nobody should ever continue aging and not learn anything, whether it be from an experience, another person, through literature, or even by some sort of formal lesson. My age has been part of the inspiration for this book, I have learned so much in the years I've been given, and I am beyond thankful.

# PATIENCE WILL BRING VALUE TO YOUR LIFE

In a world where we can acquire most things in no time flat, it can be difficult to accept the fact that some things require us to wait. Patience is a quality that everyone can benefit from because it assists with comprehension and clarity. For example, early in life we tend to learn more effectively when we are allowed to be in environments that understand that we are brand new blank canvases that are slowly developed into unique masterpieces but require a variety of individuals to be patient with us so we can grasp the concept of life. As for the clarity piece, patience allows capable adults to slowly and effectively think through situations, oftentimes avoiding actions that could later be a regret. As a military service member and a former police officer, I have experienced several situations that required me to be level-headed and patient with individuals who were blatantly disrespectful and uncooperative as I performed my duties. What I learned from these experiences is that people will behave recklessly and belligerently, and if you react impulsively, it only makes the situation worse and effects your credibility.

I consider myself a calm, logical, and rational being, but it took some time for me to develop that side of me. As a former athlete, I've always had a competitive nature, and a tenacity that wasn't always accepted. Although I am that same person to my core, I am a more polished version of myself. Evolution is a life necessity. Please remember to be patient with your children, your loved ones, the people you've agreed to spend a considerable amount of life with, and even those you don't know.

## LESSON 9

# Maintaining Your Health is a Lifelong Task

This is a topic I bring up in a lot of my content. It is extremely important to me that I stay on top of my fitness and health, because I want to maintain my ability to freely maneuver as I age. I think it helps a lot that I grew up with the drive, work ethic, and interest in working out and being active. At first, the entire extent of my wanting to stay fit was the aesthetic, as well as because it was necessary for me to maintain my competitiveness as an athlete. Now, the aesthetic is still very much a part of my fitness journey, but more importantly I enjoy the feeling of being in the gym and understanding what I'm doing, I have a routine that I stick with that empowers me to remain consistent, it is refreshing to look and feel great in my clothes, and I am eligible to seek out careers in service that interest me without difficulty. Additionally, I am not super familiar with my extended family history, and I take interest in staying as healthy as I can on my own, without the interference of medication and other invasive instances. Getting older should not be an ailment, but more like an opportunity to consistently be better. I can argue that I'm getting better as I get older, and I love that for me!

# EDUCATION IS LIFE!

Learning is a life skill that should never stop. Education is associated with pursuing a degree, but it is also pursuing the understanding of life skills. I am someone who truly enjoys the challenge of earning degrees, because I think it gives me a chance to exercise my mental capacity, it introduces new concepts and/or reintroduces old ones that I may understand better in my current state, and I just enjoy being able to add to my stack of credentials. However, learning new things about people and cultures outside of mine contribute to my growth as well. I've also learned quite a bit about people in general as it relates to race relations, how it feels to be in authority and to be a subordinate. I've also learned how to differentiate between personal and professional relationships, and more times than not I do not make acquaintances with people I work with because you never fully know the intentions of others. I like to be pleasant in the workspace, but I also understand that professionalism should stand firm and constant. As I continue to meet people and encounter situations, I come across things I hadn't considered before and sometimes retreat into my own space to think; although I enjoy being close to a select few, I am someone who also enjoys my solitude. Be a life learner, never be too good to accept a word of advice.

# Outgrowing People and Circumstances is a Thing

Holding on to people and places will put us behind in life sometimes. It's comforting to be around familiar places and things and be amongst people you know; however, it is important to see beyond familiarity. But consider this, have you ever experienced leaving home to go to school, or left to join the military, or took a job someplace away from home, or done anything of the sort? Then, on a beak, you visited home and expected to have this magical feeling come over you because you're excited to be back home!... Then, you realize, nothing has changed, and you weren't missing anything. I recently discovered the acronym FOMO (Fear of Missing Out), and it sums up this entire idea I'm trying to convey in this section. The idea of missing out on things we believe we should be a part of can be mentally halting. Our perception of what things mean to us is a driving factor for accepting less than desired outcomes. It's perfectly fine to adore things from the past and maintain relationships with "homegirls" and old friends but be sure that closed mindedness and pessimism is not attached to their ideology. A growth mindset is valuable, attempt to be the best YOU possible. Nostalgia feels good, but sometimes a little goes a long way; a little taste of the past can be good enough to get you back focused on your current life routines.

# When Something is For You, Whomever or Whatever Has Successfully Thwarted Your First Attempt Will Never Prevail in the End

I know there is a saying that goes, "What is meant for you, nobody can take away"; but unfortunately, that's not totally true. I agree with the concept that if something is meant for you it will work out at some point. However, people in certain positions will negatively impact opportunities for you, simply because they have the authority to. Even though it is professionally illegal to be bias against someone based on racial characteristics, gender, and other individualities, does not mean that it is not still done to people. The real world has some hard truths to swallow, but it is imperative that you never give up on the things that you want for yourself. Sometimes we must try things over, and over, and over again until it is our turn. I have lots of motivational and mental endurance, so I have never been dissuaded from continuously pursuing my goals. When in the pursuit of success be intense and methodical. If you have life, there is a chance to WIN!

## LESSON 13

# Don't be Embarrassed, Be Better

Sometimes failure deters us from doing things we are interested in. Or, when we go through things in our personal life, like a breakup, after we've shown lengths of happiness and promise to others, we may feel a sense of embarrassment and shame. I think we should start focusing on the lesson learned, and not what it looks like to others. It takes maturity and confidence to not care so much what others think. Embarrassment is only because of a fixation on what others think of you. I won't say that just because you are aware of others' opinions of you, means you are wrong, because taking that in could lead to character development. What I am saying is, allowing someone's opinion of you control you out of fear is silly and unbecoming. I have always made very strategic and guided moves when it comes to my professional endeavors, but sometimes in my personal life I have made exceptions for the men I've decided to date. Now, not that I think business and personal relationships are the same, but I do think there are some similarities. As I have gotten older, I have taken more of a business-like approach to dating because I have certain standards that have been added to the list based on past experiences and general accumulated knowledge over the years. I've not been embarrassed about a relationship that didn't work out in years, simply because I am in control of what I want to do in that area of my life, and I am so much better after these experiences. I am better than I was just two years ago, and I only plan to continue making better more informed decisions.

# Living a Strict Life Is Good, But Be Able to Enjoy More Times Than Not

I love to have order in my life. I am someone who lives by the book in terms of structure; some might label me as "straight-laced". I've always thought of things as being in order or having a system of steps to follow in order to reach a goal. This has worked for me in many different areas of my life, and I think I'll always be this type of person. But I do think it is very important to live a little and leave an opening for impromptu fun. Having a sense of spontaneity can be good for everyone, opening the mind and body for new opportunities, or possibly building more interesting relationships with friends and/or intimate partners. I have learned over time that being extremely strict can have the effect of making one appear rigid, close-minded, and dare I say… Boring.

It may not seem like that big of a deal if it is not something you've sat and thought over, but I do think it is relevant in several ways. Careers take over our lives sometimes, especially if we are thriving and successful at what we're doing, it is easy to get priorities out of order. Family life can become routine and begin to feel draining and redundant. Marriages I assume can begin to feel stale because people fail to give them the same care and attention they once did, leading to frustration and even regret. I'm far from an expert when it comes to these topics, but I have experienced many of the things I talk about personally, or I have witnessed from others what I don't want for myself. Paying attention and learning from the experiences of others is a helpful way to avoid some mistakes. The main message I want to get out is that life is not supposed to be so serious all the time, the idea of leisure and the ability to live it exist because it should be practiced. Live it up in more ways than one, and appreciate the ability to have fun!

# WE DON'T HAVE TO AGREE, WE JUST HAVE TO FIND WAYS TO MAINTAIN CIVILITY

I have learned that people disagree a lot! And that is okay. People may disagree on aspects of relations, parenting, politics, societal values and norms, and just have all-around differing viewpoints. I think the problem that people have is they can't disagree and be okay that they just don't think the same. People have the misconception that to live life alongside others, everyone must think the same to have peace. I believe one of the benefits of having opposing views is the fact that it introduces a variety of perspectives. People's experiences derive from the way they're raised, or maybe based on a life-changing event, or even due to the community they were brought up in as it relates to race or class. I aspire to be open-minded. I have my own opinions, and I do not have a problem interacting with people who don't think like me. Although I'm open, I am also okay distancing myself from people and situations that make me feel uneasy or hostile. I never said that you should accept everything. However, you should be able to disagree in a healthy fashion. I want it to be known that protecting yourself from spiteful, mean, rude, difficult, and angry people is certainly a great thing to do. Being a mature, civil being in an adverse situation can save you some regret, it allows you to avoid certain consequences later most times. Think before you act. Analyze the situation. Be as direct as you possibly can and always stand your ground. Disagreeing is a part of life. Be okay with conflict but be able to navigate it gracefully.

## LESSON 16

# NEVER SUCCUMB TO INTIMIDATION

Being bold and ferocious is one of my personal life pillars. The book I wrote prior to this one is all about '*Cultivating Ferocity*', which is also the title of the book. Having confidence is a necessary tool to navigate this life. This is true even more so in times of adversity. Everyone will experience a time in their life when they encounter something so trying, it discourages them or makes them question themselves in some way. Never let a bad experience deter you from something you feel strongly about accomplishing. For example, consider the current climate in society. There are changes being made that could affect everyone financially, or maybe an opportunity that was originally available has taken a halt or been rescinded due to policies being changed. Even after these challenges, it is up to YOU to maintain confidence, optimism, determination, and effort towards the dream and desires you have for yourself.

Being told no has never broken my efforts to get the things that I want for myself. I may have taken a break in order to regroup and create a different plan, but I have never given up on myself. I would be dishonest if I said that I have never been intimidated throughout the process of pursuing different careers for positions that seemed to hold a great amount of authority. However, it was simply an opportunity to gain more knowledge and experience in leadership and whatever else would contribute to my bringing more to the position. Fast forward to now, I am certain that I am competitive and qualified for the things that I see for myself. Keeping in mind that all great things don't happen on the first try, I go full force to do my best to heighten the chances that they do. Either way, live ferociously and in the now.

# KNOW YOUR POSITION IN PEOPLE'S LIFE

A hard lesson to learn is that we often incorrectly gauge our worth to other people. It could be a relative, a spouse or life partner, an employer, a friend, or even a business partner. It is impossible to attempt to impress upon others what they should think or feel about you. It could be an extremely hurtful experience, but as long as God decides, you will live to see another day. I am a very sentimental person, I cherish those I consider near and dear to me, I take pride in maintaining healthy close relationships, I enjoy the experience of seeing others succeed, and I take the relationships I enter seriously. Unfortunately, I have experienced the hurt of not being as high on the list with people I felt I had an intense connection with. I have learned that the only person I can always count on, is ME. Win or lose, high or low, success or failure, pass or fail. This realization is something I hold dear to me, because it allows me to escape a pattern of lingering disappointment and spiraling into a depressive state. Do for others because you want to, and it will bring you joy to do so. Share things that you feel could help someone else because you want to. Donate to a cause or loan someone money because you decided you can afford it, and it is something you want to do. With that, understand that nobody is obligated to do the same for you. Nobody has to go out of their way to help you, just because you helped them. Love the person or people you choose to love, and don't be shocked if they won't reciprocate. Just learn from the experience and be prepared next time. Sometimes we just don't matter as much to others as we believe we do, and that's okay. Move on and act accordingly.

# Don't Dwell on Being Liked, Focus on Doing Your Very Best

The world is full of people who come from all over the world. These people have upbringings that differed from yours. They have beliefs instilled in them from their parents who grew up in a different era, where their ideology was developed by the people and world around them. All of this to say, you are a unique being that everyone may not gravitate towards, and it is okay to stay in your realm and not be liked. It is not your job to be liked, it is your job to find your personal purpose and thrive within it. Thankfully, when it comes to people out in the world, I don't have the issue of being a people pleaser and I can accept not being the "favorite". However, I am a work in progress when it comes to wanting to over perform for people who are close to me. In relationships, I have gone above and beyond to make people feel special whether they did the same for me or not. As I have lived more life, I realize that this is unacceptable and unfair to me. Once you begin the habit of doing things for people and they know that they do not have to give you the same in return, the way they treat you becomes as though you are supposed to do for them; they expect all the reward with no effort. As difficult as it may be, it is important to pull away from this dynamic and treat people and situations accordingly. If things fall apart as a result, it is apparent that you may not have been as liked as you thought by the person you trusted the most.

I have also learned this lesson by living through it as a military member. Although race should not matter when navigating professionally, it most certainly does. Most individuals are visibly the race they fall under. As a leader in service, sometimes you have to work twice as hard to prove yourself to others who feel like you do not belong, when in actuality you are more qualified than they could ever hope to be. I care about what people think about me professionally, but personally I don't have the motivation to perform for people I would never even encounter if my career choice didn't bring us to a common place. I no longer feel the need to do more than I need to, because as long as I am providing quality work and showing up at the right place and time, on time and with the proper attitude, I cannot control what happens after that. My life goal is not to be liked. It does feel nice to be liked by others, it makes things easier. But I understand that the things I see for my life may require me to have to be unliked by others, whether it's because I won't settle for mediocrity or indulge in people who have no drive, or because I don't have the patience for experiences that don't better me as a person. Your life is all about you, your personal story that can only be authored by you. Writing it on paper and living it out are very different. Ideas written down on paper without action is not very useful. Be your best self, always.

# EVERY CONNECTION IS NOT ABOUT LOVE

I love the idea of romanticism. I enjoy the thought of finding a man who loves me, us getting married, having a family, and living happily ever after... Well, as beautiful as that sounds, and as romantic as that may be, I understand that every man I meet is not a potential love connection. As a younger woman, I would meet a man and dissect him. I would think about all the things I wanted, and I would project that energy onto him. I would fantasize about us living together, going on beautiful vacations, meeting each other's families, and just being fully intertwined in each other's lives. With age I have learned that people are not always who you think they are, including yourself. Most people know about the honeymoon stage, and boy can it be a whirlwind. The newness is novelty, and everything feels so special and promising. But then, life comes rushing in and common sense returns full force. Everyone has flaws, a lot of people do things in the beginning that they don't ordinarily do, and people are just excited and willing to present themselves in a way that seems promising. It has been my experience that men are quicker to settle into a relationship and not continue putting in the effort to make their woman feel special. In short, knowing what I know now about men, I am better about looking at them through a lens of objectivity.

I consider what I want for myself, how I can provide it for myself if nobody ever comes to assist, and what I could possibly lose if I were to let someone enter my life who is unsupportive and secretly jealous. It is important to have healthy relationships that make us feel good, that provide a foundation of care and consideration, and foster support and reciprocity. I only want that type of energy in my personal orbit. Every person you meet is not supposed to be in your life forever, and that is okay. Take things and people for what they are worth, expect nothing more than what you can see, and save yourself from disappointment by not expecting what you would do from others.

# Move On

Dreams and hopes are hard to walk away from, especially when you saw something for yourself that did not come to fruition. It's also difficult to walk away from someone who you made life plans with at any point in life. I believe as you get older the ability to walk away and recover from heartbreak becomes easier. When you're young, you're all hopeful and optimistic about people being able and willing to change, instead of taking things at face value. Either way, life will be much easier when you simply move on. Move on from the failures you've held on to for years, move on from the job loss, move on from the emotional damage you've endured so that you can remain healthy and functional, and just move on from the things holding you back from your growth. It's interesting that most of the topics I cover in this book sort of revolve around the same message. But the thing about growth is that it's all relative! The one thing that has allowed me to continue striving to be my best self, is the fact that I've been given the chance to move on into my designated space in life. I am right where I need to be at all times, I believe in destiny. Once I win the battle mentally, everything else is easy. If you take nothing else from this read, please retain the sentiment that moving on is one of the most freeing events you'll ever experience in your life. The relief of releasing burdens is immaculate.

# INTELLIGENCE IS GREAT, BUT HUMILITY CONSISTENTLY WINS

Nobody likes a know-it-all. It is amazing that you are intelligent, and you have the capacity to understand concepts, and literature, or whatever else classifies you as gifted. However, if you can channel those smarts in a way that others can relate to, it may be more effective. For example, people are more inclined to do things to show off and exert their dominance over others to gain a position. But, if you can both display your geniuses in a way that will benefit you AND teach others so that they can contribute to the cause, then it shows that you are both skilled and emotionally intelligent. Being smart is awesome, but being a pretentious, unlikable, snooty person is unattractive, and most people wouldn't aspire to have that be their reputation. Humbleness is a character trait that is conducive to versatility. Meaning being humble doesn't mean that you are overly acquiescent or not capable of standing your ground, it just highlights your capacity to show your talents in a way that is present yet subtle. Being the smartest person in the room is impressive and additionally seeking ways to transfer that knowledge to others, and/or find a way to gain knowledge from others is even more impressive. You will win more when you are teachable and have a good attitude, no matter what level you have ascended to. Be the example for others and present what you would want to receive. Smart people don't just consider themselves; they think of others as well.

## LESSON 22

# FIND A LIFE QUOTE THAT INSPIRES YOU, AND LIVE BY IT!

When I was in the third grade, I remember in literature class we would read all sorts of things like short stories, break down books like 'Moby Dick', and we'd also read poems and discuss what we felt the meanings behind them were. I think around this time I discovered I really liked poetry, and I was fascinated with the different poem set-ups poets used, and I was even more intrigued with the unique language involved that told stories of people's lives and experiences. There was one poem that stood out to me as a kid, and to this day is somewhat of a mantra I live by. The poem is titled *"Dreams"* by Langston Hughes. Mr. Hughes had so many works of art that were special and meaningful, but 'Dreams' is my favorite because from the age of seven to age 33 it is still relevant to my life. Holding on to dreams is important, living a life full of things I aspire to accomplish is something that keeps me motivated and excited about both now and the future. As a kid reading that poem, I felt like it was a reminder for me to excel at all costs. I felt encouraged and nurtured by his words and the tone of what he was saying. I vividly remember keeping the textbook for that class, just so I could revisit that poem for years to come. I did not want to forget it. I wanted it to resonate throughout my being for years to come, and it surely has. Thinking back, I was very intuitive as a child, and it is very interesting to me that I remember everything that I felt and thought after reading 'Dreams'. As an adult, I just have the words speak for ME as a developed mind.

### Dreams by Langston Hughes

Hold fast to dreams
For if dreams die
Life is a broken-winged bird
That cannot fly.

Hold fast to dreams
For when dreams go
Life is a barren field
Frozen with snow.

*–Hughes (1922)*

## LESSON 23

# Avoid Lowering Standards

Life can be challenging and sometimes we must wait a bit longer for the things we want. Impatience is ingrained in society today, because there are so many options to have things expedited and delivered to your doorstep with the push of a button. Unfortunately, because we want things immediately, we may miss out on quality. Settling is not a bad thing, but only when you're settling for the best option based on your needs and desires. However, settling for anything just to say you have something is never a great option. Life may bring challenges and the one choice you've been given may be unavoidable at that time, but striving for better is where the action takes place. I am blessed to be able to acquire the things I need, as well as a lot of the things I want. I am all about saving money so that it can be accessible in the event I may need it. But I was being a little bit too frugal at one point and depriving myself of things I knew I could manage because my mindset was rigid. I am not a car person in the sense that I am up on the latest drops, but I had been eyeing a vehicle for years. It took a while for me to investigate purchasing it because I enjoyed not paying a car note and pocketing money as a result. But I felt it would be more comfortable to have more space, updated features, and more reliability with a newer SUV. I got the thing I wanted because I just wanted it, and I could afford to have it. It is okay to responsibly gift yourself with nice things; maybe even encouraged. The message I am trying to relay is that shrinking into comfort is unbecoming. Many of the examples I have in this book can be directed towards relationships. As social creatures who require interaction with others for a healthy living experience, it is paramount that we choose the best people to be around. Never accept from others what you would not provide for yourself, and accept only the best option that will stimulate your well-roundedness. Always maintain the mindset that you are worth it.

# Pay Attention to What People Show You, Not What You Think of Them

People can over promise and under deliver, but it is your job to decode the message they're conveying to you and understand the reality of the situation. I think optimism is necessary in life, but sometimes reality kicks in and we must pay attention. The option to count on others is a blessing and it feels nice to have help. However, people have a tendency to say things to sound nice and appeasing in the moment but somehow fade away when it's time to show up. Although we only have people's word to go by, I have learned to refrain from getting too excited about the words people feed me until they follow through. I am a very intentional person in everything that I affiliate myself with. Whether it be an educational or fitness goal, a favor I agreed to provide to someone, or even just setting a timer on my phone to ensure I cut off my television and get off entertainment apps on my phone so that I can go to bed at a decent hour; keep myself accountable. I don't necessarily care if someone likes me or not, but I do care about how they describe my integrity and morality. I strive to be a reliable individual because it irritates me when people are not trustworthy with things they agreed to. Paying attention to people's behavior can curve the level of disappointment you may experience; you can spot the inauthenticity upfront!

## LESSON 25

# CLOSURE IS A MYTH

It is your responsibility to establish a stopping point for things you need to remove yourself from; ONLY yours. Expecting others to provide you with "closure" is irresponsible to say the least. Others cannot provide you with the soothing you seek when it comes to the end of a relationship or anything else, because they are rarely feeling the same things as you at that moment in time. We all experience emotions that confuse and hurt us, but it is on us personally to process them adequately. If you leave your healing to someone else, you'll rarely evolve from the things you should be getting away from. There is no law set forth that states for you to move on you must first get closure, or everything moving forward will be doomed! So, because this is not a fact, relax, go through the emotions, give yourself grace, and move on to better things.

# Hobbies Are a Life Goal

Throughout life, there should always be something you enjoy doing, aspire to learn, or have maintained doing over time. Life is supposed to be enjoyable and not a constant business venture. This is an adjustment I had to make in my life to ensure that I was only catering to my professional life. I am super goal oriented, but I also realized that I needed something that was only for me and my enjoyment, and not something I was doing as a contribution to a work-related concern. I am such a curious person, and I can always find something I want to venture into. Admittedly, sometimes I can take on too much and end up not really giving some stuff the time it deserves. One hobby I plan to maintain throughout my life is going to the gym. There are so many people who feel like the gym is a chore or it's a means to an end. Personally, I like the way I feel when I am at the gym exercising and in my own zone. I've grown so much in fitness that I understand how to structure my own workouts, why the exercises are being done and the expected outcomes, and I am more aware of my body in a variety of ways. Fitness has been a journey that has slight changes over time, mostly in the way I perform for my age. I used to feel like the harder and faster you work out in the gym, the more extreme your outcome will be in terms of definition and strength. However, I've come to realize that sometimes less is more; consistency is key. In addition to my passion for fitness, I have an understanding of food and how it works for my body. My love for my gym hobby benefits my health, my confidence in my appearance, and my ability to physically perform with minimal effort. I think the next level for me would be to establish a safe and healthy fitness schedule as a pregnant person. I have always thought about how I would sustain in the event I got pregnant. That is a challenge I am looking forward to. In conclusion, find your happy place in a new venture and always have focus in something that interests you.

# Be Thankful

Sitting in solitude is one way I do a mental overview of things in my life and make time to be mentally aware of all the things I've been blessed to experience, appreciative of the skills I possess, and happy about the life I have lived and plan to live. In good times you should be thankful, but maybe more so in times of despair. Your attitude is one of the biggest factors in determining which way a situation may go; the way you thinketh, so shall it be. The saying "a mind is a terrible thing to waste" is such a powerful statement, because our entire existence aside from autonomous organs that we influence with our life choices, is controlled by our thoughts. If you think about society in its construction, it takes a certain level of mental capacity to establish things. Be thankful that your health is intact. I imagine that so many people were in sorrow on their last few moments, fantasizing about what could have been if they didn't fall ill or decide to affect their health by partaking in substance abuse. Be thankful for your ability to sustain your life financially. Having monetary resources is vital to life in our world. A lot of people complain about their jobs or their inability to receive the compensation they feel they deserve but overlook the fact that without their current income they could not live comfortably. Also, be aware that you are not supposed to be anywhere other than where you currently are in life. I believe God makes no mistakes. Do not rush to your next move in life, you never know what it comes with. Be thankful for everything that comes with your life because it is your experience to learn from.

# LOVE THE ONES CLOSE TO YOU

Life is a challenge when you are on your own. No matter how massive the amount of money you make is, or the title you hold, or even the popularity you have in life. Just because you are well-known doesn't mean you're surrounded by people who care about you. So, with that, when you have people in your circle who care about you and cherish your existence it is imperative that you celebrate them just the same. Close knit relationships are valuable because they provide the ability to communicate intimately in ways that aren't always possible otherwise. I am extremely thankful that I can speak with my parents regularly and learn the ways of being a woman from my mother. I am happy that my brother and I are closer in adulthood, and that I can see him live his life. My extended family is not always as open and available as they once were, but I do maintain a relationship with some of my elder relatives who deserve care and social interaction in their old age. I cherish people I care about, and I show it in ways I know how, such as spending time, giving gifts, providing words of encouragement, or simply sending a message when they cross my mind. There is no playbook to how to show love in a positive manner, but there are so many ways you can give someone their flowers while they are present to admire them. Step out of your comfort zone and make someone else's day. Love is one of the most contagious things in life!

# REST AND RELAXATION ARE VITAL TO GOOD HEALTH

If you are like me. You'll always have something on the agenda that you want to accomplish. It may feel like there is so little time and so much to do. But all go and no resting point is never the best option. When children are growing, they require lots of sleep and it may seem like that is all they do. But, for them to thrive and develop properly, they must get the rest they require. Well, as we age, we might not need as much sleep as a growing baby, but we also need to rest and relax to regenerate and refresh our mind and body. I remember when I was a kid, I always wondered why my parents used to say they were tired often. My thinking was "the only thing you did today was go to work, why are you so tired", lol…. Now, years later as a woman in her 30's, I absolutely understand every ounce of this feeling! I never appreciated the greatness of a nap until I grew up and had more things to do. Relaxation is just as valuable. Sometimes doing nothing is the break from the hustle and bustle of life one needs. I often must redirect myself towards putting in the effort to slow down and give attention to my time to relax. I find that when I sleep or lay down a bit longer than I plan to, when I listen to my body, I feel stronger and better able to think; less brain fog. Slow it down before life sits you down!

# Your Appearance Speaks For You First

The way you present yourself to the world will determine whether you get certain opportunities in society. Unfortunately, your expertise is often second fiddle to the way people perceive you. We can't control our race or the features that we have, but we can control the clothes we decide to wear and if they have been ironed and pressed to give off a nice, clean look. Aside from clothing, people are also apt to judge us based on our weight. As horrible as it sounds, the reality is your weight adds to your aesthetic and people will judge you based on it. Especially as a woman, I think we have a more difficult time being judged on our weight and appearance, compared to our male counterparts. Society expects women to look a certain way to measure their level of femininity and beauty. Not to say that you should be performative and do things at the behest of others, but you should want to be your best self for your own sake. Looking the part is very important as you continue to maneuver in life. Your confidence, your knowledge, and your demeanor are all a part of your appearance. Ensure that you give yourself the benefit of paying attention to detail. When you look good you feel good. Give yourself the chance to thrive; look amazing because that is all people have to go on without you saying a word.

# HUMOR IS OFTEN DISARMING

Have you noticed that when tensions are high and there is an energy of anxiousness surrounding situations, someone may try to lighten the mood with a joke? Well, sometimes that's just the thing needed to lighten the mood and have everyone take a chill pill. Now, there is an art to it that everyone is not talented enough to pull off, but oftentimes when you don't try so hard and you use a little bit of wit, the jokey joke flows right out and lands with the majority. Life itself is serious enough with so many responsibilities and things to consider, why create added stressors by being so stern and stoic 24-7. I think there is a misconception that the more serious a person is, the more reliable and professional they are. However, it has been my experience that people who never lighten up are more miserable and have less life satisfaction

## LESSON 32

# GO OUTSIDE MORE

Being outside provides the opportunity to get some fresh air and experience the beauty of nature! For me, being outdoors opens me up mentally and spiritually. I'm more aware of my surroundings and the random things I come across. I enjoy water and being around it. Some of my happiest experiences in life were those times when I was able to take a run around a body of water, or on a cruise where I could see the beautiful ocean and admire the mystery of it all, or even when I learned to confidently swim on my own without needing a flotation device nearby. Aside from my love of enjoying water outside, I love the calmness I feel when I can watch nature work. As we live our everyday lives, I think we often overlook the fact that life is taking place under our very eyes, and that animals and all other living creatures have just as much meaning. I haven't been around many babies in the past few years, as I move around a lot as a service member. But, when I was home and I was able to interact with babies in my family, I noticed that when they cried and I took them outside, there was something about that shift in the environment that calmed them. Being in the world's nest is a blessing we often take for granted, because a good majority of us have grown accustomed to staying buried inside with the air conditioner on full blast, while we lazily lounge on the couch. We've forgotten the feeling of sun-kissed skin, an enjoyable cool breeze, and the comfort of sitting under a tree's cool shade. Going outdoors can bring your life the Zen you never realized it needed. Go get some fresh air, it will make a difference!

# FIND REASONS TO BE HAPPY & CONTENT WITH LIFE, YOU NEVER KNOW WHEN THE RIDE ENDS: TIME IS LIFE'S ULTIMATE VALUE

I saved the best for last! This is one lesson I have come to realize is probably the most valuable. I am an optimist. I believe that there is always an upside in any situation. YOU are in control of creating happiness for yourself. Understanding that life is the only thing where you set things up in anticipation of the next thing happening. We are never really at ease in our security of stability. Working, worrying, parenting, being in relationships, overcoming sadness and frustration, are all things that are some people's constant, and they never attempted to fix it; they dwelled in misery. Life is a gift of time. Your time is unbeknownst to you, and if you're reading these words, you still have time. Some have not been as fortunate, they're life ended at birth or in childhood, they were taken away in adolescence, or they were involved in something that removed them from the free world which is often a very similar experience I suppose. There may be times when you feel as though your options in life are not as good as you'd like them to be but understand that you have them. If small things in your mind shifted, you could always find a reason to appreciate what you've been given in life. Time is something I have seen from a different perspective as I've aged. For example, I can clearly remember the way I felt about planning things in my twenties, compared to how I plan them now in my thirties. Before, I would have some immediacy, but it felt like a distant thing because I did not have the resources financially, and/or a plan that was sustainable enough to get it done at that time. Now, I am more aware of how to acquire certain resources, I have the life experience of maneuvering through roadblocks, and I am even more confident in how to go about my ambitions. Another thing I appreciate about where I am in life is the opportunity I've had to experience being smarter; the realization of my frontal lobe developing. I literally can tell the difference in myself from a younger woman to now. I just woke up one day, and I swear I just understood things. As we come to a close, I just want to tell you all to appreciate the fact that every day you awake and realize life is still in you, there is a chance to be happy another day! I hope you get something from this book, it is my gift to you.

Made in the USA
Monee, IL
24 June 2025

ee79ae73-19cc-41c0-922d-96750c0f28e2R02